The Surprising Purpose of *Anger*

Beyond Anger Management: Finding the Gift

A Nonviolent Communication™ presentation and workshop transcription by

Marshall B. Rosenberg, PhD

PuddleDancer
P R E S S

2240 Encinitas Blvd., Ste. D-911, Encinitas, CA 92024
email@PuddleDancer.com • www.PuddleDancer.com

For additional information:
Center for Nonviolent Communication
5600 San·Francisco Rd., NE, Suite A, Albuquerque, NM 87109
Ph: 505-244-4041 • Fax: 505-247-0414 • Email: cnvc@cnvc.org • Website: www.cnvc.org

The Surprising Purpose of Anger
Beyond Anger Management: Finding the Gift

© 2005 PuddleDancer Press
A PuddleDancer Press Book

PuddleDancer Press, Permissions Dept.
2240 Encinitas Blvd., Ste. D-911, Encinitas, CA 92024
Tel: 760-652-5754 Fax: 760-274-6400
www.NonviolentCommunication.com Email@PuddleDancer.com

Ordering Information
Please contact Independent Publishers Group,
Tel: 312-337-0747; Fax: 312-337-5985; Email: frontdesk@ipgbook.com
or visit www.IPGbook.com for other contact information and details
about ordering online

Author: Marshall B. Rosenberg, PhD
Editor: Graham Van Dixhorn, Write to Your Market, Inc.,
        www.writetoyourmarket.com
Cover and Interior Design: Lightbourne, Inc., www.lightbourne.com
Cover Photograph: Digital Vision collection from
        www.gettyimages.com

Manufactured in the United States of America

1st Printing, Fall 2005

10 9 8

978-1-892005-15-1

Contents

A Brief Introduction to NVC 1

    Anger and NVC 2
    It Works Even If Only One Person Applies It 3

Steps to Handling Our Anger 4

    The First and Second Steps 4
        Evaluating Triggers That Lead to Anger 5
        Trigger Versus Cause 7
        An Illustration of Stimulus Versus Cause of Anger 9
    The Third Step 10
        Judgments 10
        Developing a Literacy of Needs 11
    The Fourth Step 13
    Punishment and Anger 15

Killing People Is Too Superficial 16

    Workshop Interactions 19
    From Philosophical to Tactical to Practical 21
    Example of One Woman's Anger 22

Getting Understanding From Others About
  Our Feelings and Needs 27

    Enjoying the Judgment Show in Your Head 30
    Take Your Time 32

An Invitation 33

Anger Sound Bites 34

    The Four-Part Nonviolent Communication Process *36*
    Some Basic Feelings and Needs We All Have *37*

About Nonviolent Communication *38*

About PuddleDancer Press *39*

About the Center for Nonviolent Communication *40*

Trade Books From PuddleDancer Press *41*

Trade Booklets From PuddleDancer Press *43*

The Surprising Purpose of *Anger*

A Q&A Session With
Marshall B. Rosenberg, PhD

*I*n The Surprising Purpose of Anger *Marshall Rosenberg shares his unique perspective on the role anger can play in our life. He challenges us to shift from the idea that anger is something to be suppressed. Instead, anger is a gift, challenging us to connect to the unmet needs that have triggered this reaction. Rosenberg reveals common misconceptions about anger and points out that our anger is the product of thinking. A discussion of anger easily supports a better understanding of Nonviolent Communication because it touches on so many key NVC distinctions. Living from your heart, making judgment-free observations, getting clear about your feelings and needs, making clear requests, and supporting life-enriching connections all relate to how we respond to anger.*

A Brief Introduction to NVC

NVC evolved out of an intense interest I have in two questions. First, I wanted to better understand what happens to human beings that leads some of us to behave violently and exploitatively. And secondly, I wanted to better understand what kind of education serves us in the attempt to remain compassionate—which I believe is our nature—even when others are behaving violently or exploitatively.

I've found in my exploration into these two questions that three factors are very important in understanding why some of us respond violently—and some of us compassionately—in similar situations. These three are:

- First, the language that we have been educated to use.
- Second, how we have been taught to think and communicate.
- Third, the specific strategies we learned to influence ourselves and others.

I have found that these three factors play a large role in determining whether we're going to be able to respond compassionately or violently in situations. I have integrated the type of language, the kinds of thinking, and the forms of communication that strengthen our ability to willingly contribute to our own well-being and the well-being of others, into this process that I call Nonviolent Communication (NVC).

NVC focuses attention on whether people's needs are being fulfilled, and if not, what can be done to fulfill these needs. It shows us how to express ourselves in ways that increase the likelihood others will willingly contribute to our well-being. It also shows us how to receive the messages of others in ways that increase the likelihood that we will willingly contribute to their well-being.

Anger and NVC

When it comes to managing anger, NVC shows us how to use anger as an alarm that tells us we are thinking in ways that are not likely to get our needs met, and are more likely to get us involved in interactions that are not going to be very constructive for anyone. Our training stresses that *it is dangerous to think of anger as something to be repressed, or as something bad.* When we tend to identify anger as a result of something wrong with us, then our tendency is to want to repress it and not deal with anger. That use of anger, to repress and deny it, often leads us to express it in ways that can be very dangerous to ourselves and others.

Think of how many times you've read in the newspapers about serial killers and how they are described by others who have known them. A rather typical way they are described is: "He was always such a nice person. I never heard him raise his voice. He never seemed to be angry at anyone."

So in NVC we are interested in using the anger in ways that help us to get at the needs that are not being fulfilled within ourselves, that are at the root of our anger.

Many of the groups I work with around the world have witnessed the consequences of teaching that anger is something to be repressed. These groups have witnessed that when we teach that anger should be avoided, it can be used to oppress people by getting them to tolerate whatever is happening to them. However, I also have reservations about how, in response to that concern, some have advocated cultivating or "venting" of anger without understanding its roots and transforming it. Some studies have indicated that anger management programs that simply encourage participants to vent anger by, for example, beating pillows, etc., simply push the anger closer to the surface and in fact leave the participants more susceptible to express their anger later in ways that are dangerous to themselves and others.

So what we want to do as we use NVC to manage anger is to go more deeply into it, to see what is going on within us when we are angry, to be able to get at the need—which is the root of anger—and then fulfill that need. For teaching purposes, I sometimes refer to anger as similar to the warning light on the dashboard of a car—it's giving you useful information about what the engine needs. You wouldn't want to hide or disconnect or ignore it. You'd want to slow down the car and figure out what the light's trying to tell you.

It Works Even If Only One Person Applies It

It has been my experience that if I can keep my attention on anger as a warning, no matter how the other person is communicating, we remain connected. In other words, NVC works, even if only one person applies it.

It's not too hard then to keep the focus in this direction. It *can* be scary because it always requires vulnerability on our part just to nakedly say how we are and what we would like. And it can flow fairly well when both parties are trained in this process, but almost everyone that I work with is attempting to establish this flow of communication with someone who is not likely to ever come to workshops to learn how to do this. So it's very important that this process work with anyone, whether they have been trained to communicate this way or not.

One thing we certainly stress in our intensive training is how to stay with this process regardless of how other people communicate. Now, in one sense anger is a fun way to dive more deeply into NVC even if you are starting with this process for the first time. When you're angry, it brings many aspects of the NVC process into sharp focus, helping you see the difference between NVC and other forms of communication.

The NVC approach involves several steps. I will go over these steps in part by using an example of a young man in a prison in Sweden. I was working with this man in a prisoner training session, showing the participants how NVC can be used to manage their anger.

Steps to Handling Our Anger

The First and Second Steps

The first step in handling our anger using NVC is to be conscious that *the stimulus, or trigger, of our anger is not the cause of our anger.* That is to say that it isn't simply what people do that makes us angry, but it's something within us that responds to what they do that is really the cause of the anger. This requires us to be able to separate the trigger from the cause.

In the situation with the prisoner in Sweden, the very day that we were focusing on anger, it turned out that he had a lot of anger in relationship to the prison authorities. So he was very glad to have us there to help him deal with anger on that day.

I asked him what it was that the prison authorities had done that was the stimulus of his anger. He answered, "I made a request of them three weeks ago, and they still haven't responded." Well, he had answered the question in the way that I wanted him to. He had simply told me what they had *done*. He hadn't mixed in any evaluation, and that is the first step in managing anger in a nonviolent way: simply to be clear what the stimulus is, but not to mix that up with judgments or evaluation. This alone is an important accomplishment. Frequently when I ask such a question, I get a response such as, "they were inconsiderate," which is a moral judgment of what they "are" but doesn't say what they actually did.

The second step involves our being conscious that the stimulus is never the cause of our anger. That is, it isn't simply what people do that makes us angry. *It is our evaluation of what has been done that is the cause of our anger.* And it's a particular kind of evaluation.

NVC is built on the premise that anger is the result of life-alienated ways of evaluating what is happening to us, in the sense that it isn't directly connected to what we need or what the people around us need. Instead, it is based on ways of thinking that imply wrongness or badness on the part of others for what they have done.

Evaluating Triggers That Lead to Anger

There are four ways that we can evaluate any anger triggers that occur in our lives. In the case of the prison officials not responding for three weeks to his request, he could have looked at the situation and taken it personally, as a rejection. Had he done that, he would not have been angry. He might have felt hurt, he might have felt discouraged, but he wouldn't have felt angry.

As a second possibility, he could have looked within himself and seen what his needs were. Focusing directly on our needs is a way of thinking that is most likely to get them met, when we are on them. Had he been focused directly on his needs, as we will see later, he would not have been angry. He might have felt scared, which it turned out he was when he got in touch with his needs.

Or another possibility: We could look at things in terms of what needs the other party was experiencing that led them to behave as they did. This kind of understanding of the needs of others does not leave us feeling angry. In fact, when we are really directly connected with the needs of others—at the point at which we understand their needs—we are not really in touch with any feelings within ourselves, because our full attention is on the other person.

The fourth way that we can look at things, which *we will find always at the base of anger*, is to think in terms of *the wrongness of other people for behaving as they did*. In NVC, whenever we feel angry, we recommend saying to ourselves, "I'm feeling angry because I am telling myself _____," and then to look for the kind of life-alienated thinking going on inside our head that is the cause of our anger.

In the case of the prisoner, when he told me that he was angry and that the trigger for his anger was that the prison officials hadn't responded for three weeks to his request, I asked him to look inside and tell me what the cause of his anger was. He seemed confused, and he said to me: "I just told you the cause of my anger. I made a request three weeks ago and the prison officials still haven't responded to it."

I told him: "Now, what you told me was the trigger for your anger. In our previous sessions I've tried to clarify for you that it's never simply the trigger that creates our anger. The cause is what we're looking for. So I'd like you to tell me how you are interpreting their behavior, how you are looking at it, that is causing you to be angry."

He was very confused at this point. He was like many of us: He had not been trained to be conscious of what was going on within himself when he was angry. So I had to give him a little help to get an idea of what I meant by how to just stop and listen to the kind of thoughts that might be going on inside of us that are always at the core of anger.

After a few moments he said to me: "OK, I see what you mean. I'm angry because I'm telling myself it isn't fair, that isn't a decent way to treat human beings. They are acting as though they are important, and I'm nothing." And he had several other such judgments that were floating rapidly through his head. Notice he initially said it was simply their behavior that was making him angry. But it was really all of these thoughts that he had within himself that were making him angry, any one of which could have created his anger. But he was ready with a whole series of such judgments, "They're not fair; they're not treating me right." All such judgments are the cause of anger.

Once we had identified this, he said to me, "Well, what's wrong with thinking that way?" And I said: "I'm not saying there's anything wrong with thinking that way. I'd just like you to be conscious that it's thinking that way which is the cause of your anger. And we don't want to mix up what people do—the trigger—with the cause of anger."

Trigger Versus Cause

Now, this is very hard for many of us to keep straight: to not mix up the trigger, or stimulus, of our anger with the cause of our anger. The reason that that's not easy for us is that we may have been educated by people who use guilt as a primary form of trying to motivate us. When you want to use guilt as a way of manipulating people, you need to confuse them into thinking that the trigger is the cause of the feeling. In other words, if you want to use guilt with somebody, you need to communicate in a way that indicates that your pain is being caused simply by what they do. In other words, their behavior is not simply the stimulus of your feelings; it's the cause of your feelings.

If you are a guilt-inducing parent, you might say to a child, "It really hurts me when you don't clean up you room." Or if you are a guilt-inducing partner in an intimate relationship, you might say to your partner, "It makes me angry when you go out every night of the week." Notice in both of those examples, the speaker is implying that the stimulus is the cause of the feelings. You make me feel. That makes me feel. I'm feeling _____ because you _____.

If we are to manage anger in ways that are in harmony with the principles of NVC, it's important for us to be conscious of this key distinction: *I feel as I do* because *I am telling myself thoughts about the other person's actions that imply wrongness on their part.* Such thoughts take the form of judgments such as, "I think the person is selfish, I think the person is rude, or lazy, or manipulating people, and they shouldn't do that." Such thoughts take either the form of direct judgment of others or indirect judgments expressed through such things as, "I'm judging this person as thinking only they have something worth saying." In these latter expressions, it's implicit that we think what they're doing isn't right.

Now that's important, because if I think this other person is making me feel this way, it's going to be hard for me not to imagine punishing them. We show people it's never what the other person does; it's how you see it; how you interpret it. And if people would follow me around in my work, they would get some very significant learning in this area.

I worked a lot in Rwanda. I often worked with people who had members of their family killed, and some are so angry all they can do is wait for vengeance. They're furious. Other people in the same room had the same family members killed, maybe had even more killed, but they are not angry. They have strong feelings, but not anger. They have feelings that lead them to want to prevent this from ever happening to others again, but not to punish the other side. We want people to see that it's how we look at the situation that *creates* our anger, not the stimulus itself.

We try to get people to see that when you're angry, it's because your consciousness is under the influence of the kind of language we all learned: That the other side is evil or bad in some way. It's that thinking that is the cause of anger. When that thinking is going on, we show people not how to push it down and deny the anger or deny the thinking, but to transform it into a language of life, into a language in which you are much more likely to create peace between yourself and whoever acted in the way that stimulated your anger.

We talk first about how to get conscious of this internalized thinking that's making you angry and how to transform that into what needs of yours have not been met by what the other person has done, and then how to proceed from that consciousness to create peace again between you and that person.

The first step in expressing our anger, managing it in harmony with NVC, is to identify the stimulus for our anger without confusing it with our evaluation. The second step is to be conscious that it is our evaluation of people—in the form of judgments that imply wrongness—that causes our anger.

An Illustration of Stimulus Versus Cause of Anger

I was working one time in a correctional school for delinquents, and I had an experience that really helped me learn the lesson that it is never the stimulus that causes the anger. There is always, between the trigger and the anger, some thought process that is going on.

On two successive days, I had remarkably similar experiences, but each day I had quite different feelings in reaction to the experience. The experience in both situations involved my being hit in the nose, because on two successive days, I was involved in breaking up a fight between two different students, and in both cases as I was breaking up the fight, I caught an elbow in the nose.

On day one, I was furious. On day two, even though the nose was even sorer than it was on the first day, I wasn't angry. Now, what was the reason I would be angry in response to the stimulus on day one, but not on day two?

First of all, in the first situation if you had asked me right after I had been hit in the nose why I was angry, I would have had trouble finding the thought that was making me angry. I probably would have said, "Well I'm obviously angry because the child hit me in the nose." But that wasn't the cause. As I looked at the situation later, it was very clear to me that the child whose elbow hit me in the nose on day one was a child that I was thinking of before this incident in very judgmental terms. I had in my head a judgment of this child as a spoiled brat. So as soon as his elbow hit my nose, I'm angry—it seemed that just as the elbow hit I was angry—but between that stimulus and the anger this image flashed within me of this child being a spoiled brat. Now, that all happens very fast, but it was the image of "spoiled brat" that made me angry.

On the second day, I carried quite a different image into the situation of that child. That child I saw more as a pathetic creature than a spoiled brat, and so when the elbow caught my nose, I wasn't angry. I certainly felt physical pain, but I wasn't angry, because a different image of a child in great need of support flashed through my mind rather than the judgmental image "spoiled brat" which caused the anger.

These images happen very quickly and they can easily trick us into thinking that the stimulus is the cause of our anger.

The Third Step

The third step involves looking for the need that is the root of our anger. This is built on the assumption that we get angry because our needs are not getting met. The problem is that we're not in touch with our needs. Instead of being directly connected to our need, we go up to our head and start thinking of what's wrong with other people for not meeting our needs. The judgments we make of other people—which cause of our anger—are really *alienated expressions of unmet needs.*

Judgments

Over the years, I have come to see that these kinds of judgments of others that make us angry are not only alienated expressions of our needs, but at times they look to me like they are suicidal, tragic expressions of our needs. Instead of going to our heart to get connected to what we need and are not getting, we direct our attention to judging what is wrong with other people for not meeting our needs. When we do this, a couple of things are likely to happen.

First, our needs are not likely to get met, because when we verbally judge other people as wrong in some way, these judgments usually create more defensiveness than learning or connection. At the very least, they don't create much cooperation. Even if people do things we would like them to do after we have judged them as wrong or lazy or irresponsible, they will take these actions with an energy that we will pay for. We will pay for it because when we are angry as a result of judging people—and we express these judgments to them either verbally or through our nonverbal behavior—they pick up that we are judging them as wrong in some way. Even if people then do what we would like them to do, they are likely to be motivated more out of fear of being punished, fear of being judged, out of their guilt or shame, than out of compassion in relation to our needs.

When we are using NVC, we remain conscious at all times that it's as important why people do what we would like them to do, as it is that they do it. So we are conscious that we only want people to do things willingly, and not do things because they think they're going to be punished, blamed, "guilted," or shamed if they don't.

Developing a Literacy of Needs

This practice requires that we develop a literacy and a consciousness of our needs. With a greater vocabulary of needs, we are able to more easily get in touch with the needs behind the judgments that are making us angry. For it's when we can clearly express our needs that others have a much greater likelihood of responding compassionately to whatever it is we would like.

Let's go back to the case of the prisoner from Sweden. After we had identified the judgments he was making that were creating his anger, I asked him to look behind the judgments and tell me what needs of his were not getting met. These unmet needs were actually being expressed through the judgments he was making of the prison officials.

This wasn't easy for him to do because when people are trained to think in terms of wrongness of others, they are often blind to what they themselves need. They often have very little vocabulary for describing their needs. It requires shifting attention away from judging outward, to looking inward and seeing what the need is. But with some help, he was finally able to get in touch with his need and he said: "Well, my need is to be able to take care of myself when I get out of prison by being able to get work. So the request that I was making of the prison officials was for training to meet that need. If I don't get that training, I'm not going to be able to take care of myself economically when I get out of prison, and I'm going to end up back in here."

Then I said to the prisoner, "Now that you're in touch with your need, how are you feeling?" He said, "I'm scared." So when we are directly connected to our need, we are *never* angry any more. The anger hasn't been repressed; the anger has been transformed into need-serving feelings.

The basic function of feelings is to serve our needs. The word *emotion* basically means to move us out, to mobilize us to meet our needs. So when we have a need for some nourishment, we have a feeling that we label as hunger, and that sensation stimulates us to move about to get our need for food taken care of. If we just felt comfortable each time we had a need for nourishment, we could starve, because we wouldn't be mobilized to get our need met.

This is the natural function of emotions, to stimulate us to get our needs met. But anger is stimulated by a diversion. We are not in touch with the needs that would naturally motivate us to want to get our needs met. The anger is created, as I've said, by thinking about the wrongness of others, which transfers this energy away from seeking to get the need met, into an energy designed to blame and punish other people.

After I pointed out to the prisoner the difference between getting in touch with his needs and the feelings that he had, he was then aware of his fear. He could see that the anger was because of the thinking about the wrongness of others. I then asked the prisoner, "Do you think you're more likely to get your needs met if, when you go in to talk to the prison officials, you are connected to your needs and the fear, or if you are up in your head judging them and angry?"

And he could see very clearly that he was much more likely to get his needs met if he were to be communicating from a position of connection to his needs, rather than separated from his needs and thinking of others in ways that implied wrongness. At the moment that he had this insight into what a different world he would be living in when he was in touch with his needs as opposed to judging others, he looked down at the floor and had about as sad a look on his face as I can recall any person ever having had. And I asked him, "What's going on?"

He said, "I can't talk about it right now." Later that day, he helped me understand what was going on in him. He came to me and said: "Marshall, I wish you could have taught me two years ago about anger what you taught me this morning. I wouldn't have had to kill my best friend."

Tragically, two years before, his best friend had done some things and he felt great rage in response to his judgments about what his friend had done. But instead of being conscious of what his needs were behind all of that, he really thought it was his friend that made him angry, and in a tragic interaction ended up killing the friend.

I'm not implying that every time we get angry we hurt somebody or kill them. But I am suggesting that every time we are angry, we are disconnected from our needs. We are up in our head thinking about the situation in a way that is going to make it very hard for us to get our needs met.

This is a very important step that I have just outlined: To be conscious of the thinking that is creating our anger. And as I said, the prisoner at first was totally oblivious to all of the thoughts that were going on within him that made him angry. The reason for this is that our thoughts go on very rapidly. Many of our thoughts go so quickly through our head that we are not even aware that they are there, and it really looks to us as though it was the stimulus that was the cause of our anger.

I have outlined three steps in managing our anger using NVC:

1) Identify the stimulus for our anger, without confusing it with the evaluation.

2) Identify the internal image or judgment that is making us angry.

3) Transform this judgmental image into the need that it is expressing; in other words, bring our full attention to the need that is behind the judgment.

These three steps are done internally—we're not saying anything out loud. We're simply becoming aware that our anger is not caused by what the other person has done, but by our judgment, and then we are looking for the need behind the judgment.

The Fourth Step

The fourth step involves what we would actually say out loud to the other person after we have transformed our anger into other feelings by getting in touch with the need behind the judgment.

The fourth step includes saying to the other person four pieces of information. First, we reveal to them the stimulus: what they have done that is in conflict with our needs being fulfilled. Secondly, we express how we are feeling. Notice we are not repressing the anger. The anger has been transformed into a feeling such as sad, hurt, scared, frustrated, or the like. And then we follow up our expression of our feelings with the needs of ours that are not being fulfilled.

And now we add to those three pieces of information *a clear, present request of what we want from the other person* in relationship to our feelings and unmet needs.

So in the situation with the prisoner, the fourth step on his part would be to go to the prison officials and say something like this: "I made a request three weeks ago. I still haven't heard from you, and I'm feeling scared because I have a need to be able to earn a living when I leave this prison, and I'm afraid that without the training, I was requesting it would be very hard for me to make a living. So I'd like you to tell me what is preventing you from responding to my request."

Notice that for the prisoner to communicate this required a lot of work on his part. He needed to be conscious of what was going on in him. He needed some help getting connected to his needs. In this situation he had me to help him, but in our training we show people how to do all of this for themselves.

When we're stimulated by another person and find ourselves starting to get angry, we need to manage that anger in the following ways.

If we're sufficiently trained in getting in touch with the need behind the judgments, we can take a deep breath and very rapidly go through the process that I led the prisoner through. In other words, as soon as we catch ourselves getting angry, we take a deep breath, stop, look inside, and ask ourselves quickly, "What am I telling myself that's making me so angry?" We quickly get in touch with the need that is behind that judgment. When we're in touch with the need we will feel in our body a shift away from anger to other kinds of feelings, and when we're at that point we can open our mouths and say to the other person what we're observing, feeling, needing, and make our requests.

This process takes practice. With sufficient practice, this process can be done in a matter of seconds. Perhaps we're fortunate enough to have friends around who can help us to get conscious about what's going on within us. If not, or until we are sufficiently trained, we can always take a time out. We can say to the person, "Time out. I need to do some work on myself right now because I'm afraid that anything I say is going to get in the way of both of us getting our needs met." At this point, we can go off by ourselves to get in touch with the needs behind our judgments that are making us angry. We can then go back into the situation.

Once we've practiced enough to handle our anger in this way, it's very often to our advantage to also show some empathic understanding of what was going on in the other person to lead them to behave as they did. If we're able to connect to this *before* we express ourselves, the advantage can be even greater.

If we're to be able to manage our anger when it comes up in the way that I'm outlining, a key part of it is this ability to both identify the judgment making us angry, and to quickly transform it into the need that is behind the judgment. We can develop our ability to do this quickly enough to do it in real situations if we can practice identifying judgments and translating them into needs.

An exercise I'd recommend is to list the kind of judgments that are likely to go on inside of you when you are angry. You might want to think of the most recent time that you have gotten angry, and ask yourself and write down what you were telling yourself that was making you angry.

When you have made an inventory of the kind of things you tell yourself in different situations that make you angry, you might then go back over this list and ask yourself, "What was I needing that was being expressed through that judgment?" And the more time we spend making these translations from judgments into needs, the more it will help us follow these procedures for expressing anger more quickly in real-life situations.

Punishment and Anger

I would like to add to this discussion of anger the concept of punishment. The kind of thinking that leads us to be angry is thinking that implies that people deserve to suffer for what they've done. In other words, I'm talking about the moralistic judgments we make of other people that imply wrongness, irresponsibility, or inappropriateness. At their root, all of these kinds of judgments imply that people shouldn't have done what they did, and they deserve some form of condemnation or punishment for doing it.

I believe that we'll see that punishment never can really get our needs met in a constructive way if we can ask ourselves two questions. The first question is; *what do we want the other person to do differently than what they are now doing?* If we ask only this question, at times punishment seems to work, because we may be able to get a child to stop hitting his sister if we punish him for doing it. I say it *seems to* work, because often the very act of punishing people for what they do in fact stimulates such antagonism that they continue to do it out of resentment or anger. They continue to do it longer than they would have done had there not been punishment.

But if we add a second question, I'm confident that we will then see that punishment never works in the sense of getting our needs met, for reasons that we won't be sorry for later. The second question is, *what do we want the other person's reasons to be for doing what we want them to do?*

When we ask that question, I think we will see that we never want other people to do things because they are afraid of punishment. We don't want people to do things out of obligation or duty, or out of guilt or shame, or to buy love. With some consciousness, I'm confident we would each see that we only want people to do things if they can do it willingly, because they clearly see how it's going to enrich life if they do. Any other reason for doing things is likely to create conditions that make it harder for people in the future to behave in a compassionate way toward one another.

Killing People Is Too Superficial

Part of my objective is to show how the process of Nonviolent Communication will help us to fully express our anger. This is very important to make clear with many of the groups that I work with, because most of the time I'm invited into different countries, it's to work with groups that feel that they have been very oppressed, discriminated against, and they want to increase the power that they have to change the situation. Very often such groups are a bit worried when they hear the term *Nonviolent Communication*, because very often in their history they have been exposed to various religions and other trainings that have taught them to stifle their anger, to calm down and accept whatever is happening. As a consequence, they are rather worried about anything that tells them that their anger is bad, or is something to be gotten rid of. It's a great relief for them when they come to see this and really trust that the process I'm talking about in no way wants us to stifle our anger, to repress it, to force it down. Instead, NVC is really a way of fully expressing the anger.

Now, I've said this before: To me, killing people is too superficial.

To me, any kind of killing, blaming of other people, punishing, or hurting other people is a very superficial expression of our anger. We want something much more powerful than killing or hurting people physically or mentally. That's too weak. We want something much more powerful than that to fully express ourselves. The first step that I will suggest in expressing our anger fully using Nonviolent Communication is to totally divorce the other person from any responsibility for our anger. As I've covered, this means getting out of our consciousness any kind thinking that he, she, they made me angry when they did that. When we think that way, I believe we're very dangerous. And we're not likely to fully express our anger. Instead, we're likely to superficially express anger by blaming or punishing the other person.

I show prisoners who want to punish others for what they do that vengeance is a distorted cry for empathy. That when we think we need to hurt others, what we really need is for these other people to see how we have been hurt and to see how their behavior has contributed to our pain. But most of the prisoners I have worked with have never gotten that kind of empathy from someone who has wronged them. Making the other people suffer is the best they can think of to do to find relief from their own pain.

I was demonstrating this once to a prisoner who told me he wanted to kill this man. I said, "I'll bet you I could show you something that would be sweeter than vengeance."

And the prisoner said: "No way man, I'll tell you the only thing that's kept me alive in this last two years in prison is thinking of getting out and getting this guy for what he did to me. That's the only thing in the world I want. They're gonna put me back in here and that's OK. All I want to do is get out and really hurt this guy."

I said, "I'll bet you I can show you something more delicious than that."

"No way man."

"Would you give me some time?" (I liked this guy's sense of humor. He said, "I got plenty of time, man," and he was going to be there for a while. That's why I like working with prisoners: They're not running off to appointments.) Anyway, I said, "Now what I'd like to show you is another option to hurting people. I'd like you to play the role of the other person."

Prisoner: OK.

MBR [in prisoner's role]: It's the first day I'm out of prison. I find you. The first thing I do is I grab you.

Prisoner: That's a good start

MBR: I put you in a chair and now I say, I'm gonna tell you some things and I want you to tell me back what you heard me say. You got that?

Prisoner [in other person's role]: But I can explain it!

MBR: Shut up. Did you hear what I said? I want you to tell me back what you hear me say.

Prisoner: OK.

MBR: I took you into my house and treated you as a brother, and gave you everything for eight months, and then you did what you did to me. I was so hurt I could hardly stand it. [I had heard the prisoner talk about this several times so it is not hard for me to play his role.]

Prisoner: But I can explain it!

MBR: Shut up. Tell me what you heard.

Prisoner: After all you had done for me, you felt really hurt. You would have liked something else besides what happened.

MBR: And then, do you know what it's like for the next two years to be angry day and night so that nothing would satisfy me, except thoughts of hurting you?

Prisoner: So it really got your whole life screwed up so that all you could do was be consumed with anger for two years.

So we kept this going for about another few minutes, and then this man was very emotionally moved and he said, "Stop, stop, you're right. That's what I need."

The next time I went to that prison about a month later, another guy was waiting for me as I came through the gate. He was pacing back and forth and he said, "Hey Marshall, remember the last time you said that when we really think that we enjoy hurting people or we want to hurt somebody, the real need is for understanding for how we've suffered?"

I said, "Yeah, I remember that."

"Would you go over that again today real slow? I'm getting out of here in three days, and if I don't get this clear, somebody's gonna get hurt."

So my prediction is anybody that enjoys hurting others is being exposed to a lot of violence themselves, psychological or otherwise. And they need empathy for the enormous pain that they're feeling.

Workshop Interactions

Again, the first step we need to get into our consciousness is that *what other people do is never the cause of how we feel.* What is the cause of how we feel? It's my belief that how we feel is a result of how we interpret the behavior of others at any given moment. If I ask you to pick me up at six o'clock and you pick me up at six thirty, how do I feel? Depends on how I look at it. That you were thirty minutes later than you said you would be doesn't make me feel whatever I feel, it's how I choose to interpret it. Now, if I choose to put on what I call judging ears, they're perfect for playing the game of who's right, who's wrong, who's at fault. When you put these ears on you'll find somebody at fault.

[Marshall is asked a question by an audience member.]

Man: So, you're saying it's how we interpret their behavior, what meaning we ascribe to it that causes our feelings?

MBR: Exactly. That's it: how we interpret the behavior is one part of our feelings.

There's another connection to feelings and that's this other choice. We can put on these other ears, NVC ears, but now when we put on these ears our thinking does not go to who's at fault. We do not go up to our head and make a mental analysis of the wrongness on either our part or the other person's part.

These ears help us connect to life, to the life that is going on within ourselves. And to me the life that is going on within our self can be most clearly revealed or grasped by looking at what our needs are. What are my needs in this situation? When I am connected to my needs I have strong feelings, but never anger, never anger. Anger is a result of life-alienated thinking, thinking that is disconnected from what my needs are. Anger says I have gone up to my head and have chosen to analyze the wrongness of the other person, and I'm disconnected from my needs. My needs are really the stimulus of what's going on, of my feeling of anger right now. But I am not conscious of what I need, my consciousness is on what's wrong with the other person for not meeting my needs.

Again, if I connect to the other person's needs I will never feel angry. I won't be *repressing* my anger, I simply won't feel it. I'm suggesting that how we feel is a result each moment of which of these four options we choose: Do we choose to go up to our head and judge the other person? Do we choose to go up to our head and judge our self? Do we choose to connect empathically with the other person's needs? Or do we choose to connect empathically with our needs?

It is that choice that determines our feelings. That's why Nonviolent Communication requires a very important word come after the word "because"—the word "I," not the word, "you." For instance, "I feel angry because *I* ___." This reminds us that what we feel is not because of what the other person did, but the choice I made.

Remember that I see all anger as a result of life-alienated, violence-provocative thinking. I think all anger is righteous in this sense: To fully express the anger means putting our entire consciousness on the need that isn't getting met. There is a need that isn't getting met in there. That's righteous; I mean we have a *right* to the feeling in the sense that a need is not getting met. We have to get that need met. We need the energy to motivate us get the need met. I'm suggesting that anger distorts that energy away from the direction of fulfilling the needs into punitive action, and in that sense it's a destructive energy.

From Philosophical to Tactical to Practical

Let me show you that what I'm talking about is more tactical than philosophical. To explain what I mean by tactical, let's go back to that prisoner example I gave you. I wasn't trying to sell the NVC process to him on philosophical principles, but tactical principles.

So, when he said they didn't respond to his request and I said, "OK, so what made you angry?" And he said: "I told you. They didn't respond to my request." I said: "Stop. Don't say I felt angry because *they* . . . stop and become conscious of what you're telling yourself that's making *you* so angry." But he wasn't of the philosophical or psychological background where he was used to sorting out what's going on inside.

So, I said: "Stop. Slow down. Just listen. What's going on inside?" And then it came out: "I'm telling myself that they have no respect for human beings. They're a bunch of cold, faceless bureaucrats." And he was going to go on, I said: "Stop, that's enough, that's enough. That's why you're angry." Then I said to the prisoner: "Now, it's that kind of thinking on your part making you feel very angry. Now, focus your attention on your needs. What are you needs in this situation?" He thought for a while and he said to me: "Marshall, I need the training I was requesting. If I don't get that training, as sure as I'm sitting here I'm going to end up back in this prison when I get out."

Woman: What you're saying makes sense to me but I feel like it requires being so superhuman on my part. It seems like the anger is so instantaneous and to actually be able to think through these different steps seems to require me to be much bigger than I am.

MBR: All it requires is to shut up. See, I don't see that's so super heroic. All it requires is to shut up and neither say anything intended to blame the other person at that moment nor take any actions to punish the other person. So, stop and do nothing except breathe and take these steps. First—and it's a big step—just shut up.

Woman: But, in your example when you're waiting a half an hour for a person to get there, I mean, they don't have to be there, and I'm already stewing, thinking, you know, "I can't believe he didn't pick me up." "Doesn't he ever remember anything I ask," and on and on and on.

MBR: What I'm saying is there's something you could be doing during that time to relieve yourself that will also increase the likelihood that you'll get your needs met. If you do these steps that we're talking about, you will have something you can say when he gets there or she gets there that is more likely to get them to be on time the next time. I hope I can make it clear so it doesn't seem superhuman. Superhuman is to try to suppress the anger, to try to push it down.

What we're really aiming for here is to keep our attention connected to life moment by moment. We connect to the life that's going on in us, what our needs are at this moment, and focus our attention on the life that's going on in other people.

Example of One Woman's Anger

Woman #2: The situation I faced is one where I was in a conversation with someone and a third person joined the conversation and started addressing the other person without me. And he made a comment to the effect that they preferred people in their community to be white.

MBR: Yes.

Woman #2: So, I felt angry because I wasn't getting my need met to continue to enjoy the conversation I was having.

MBR: Now, hold on, I doubt that, I doubt that that's why you got angry. See, I don't think we get angry because our needs aren't getting met. I'll bet you got angry because you had some thoughts about that other person at that moment. So, I'd like you to be conscious right now about what were you telling yourself that made you so angry about that person. So, here's a person that says I'd rather have only white people here and they address somebody else rather than you and you felt angry because why? Because you told yourself what?

Woman #2: Well, I told myself, What's this person doing, taking over the conversation that I was already having?

MBR: Think behind the question, 'What is this person doing?' What do you think of a person for doing that?

Woman #2: What do I think of him?

MBR: Yeah.

Woman #2: Well, it's not a good thought.

MBR: But I think it's in there. I'm not trying to make you have certain thoughts. I'm just wanting to make you conscious of what I predict is in there. It's probably going on so fast.

Woman #2: No, right away I was feeling left out.

MBR: Well, that's coming closer. So, you interpreted him as leaving you out. See, notice how the image left out is not a feeling.

Woman #2: I see.

MBR: It's an interpretation. It's like abandoned, "I'm feeling abandoned." "I'm feeling unnoticed." So, it's really more an image; you have this image of being left out. And what else was going on there?

Woman #2: I think it was more than an image because they were making eye contact and talking to the other person, and in that exchange they were not talking to me.

MBR: But, I think there are twenty different ways we could look at that, of which leaving you out is only one. There are many other possible ways of interpreting that. And I'm saying each one is going to have a big impact of how you feel. So, let's slow down again. What other thoughts were going on in you that made you angry at that moment?

Woman #2: Well, I had thoughts associated with when somebody uses the word *white.*

MBR: Yeah, I think we're getting closer now. So, what is your image when somebody uses the word *white* in that way? Especially when they don't look at you and they look at the others?

Woman #2: What I told myself is when they say white they don't mean me.

MBR: So, they're kind of excluding you.

Woman #2: And, in fact, their behavior and body language and everything is also giving me that message.

MBR: So, you believe they are excluding you because of race? Do you have any thoughts about people who do that?

Woman #2: Yeah, a lot, I mean . . .

MBR: That's what I'm trying to get at, you see. I'm thinking it's those thoughts that got stimulated in that moment by that action and that's what made you angry.

Woman #2: I think so. I agree with what you're saying. I think it was both that and the actual fact that I was actually being excluded.

MBR: No, you weren't actually being excluded. That was an interpretation that you were being excluded. The fact, as I'm defining this observation as a fact, is that the person had eye contact with others, see that's the fact. Whether you interpret that as excluding you, whether you interpret that as racist, whether you interpret that as that person being frightened of you, these are all interpretations. The fact was he didn't look at you. The fact was he said something about white. Those are the facts. But if you interpret it as excluding, already you are going to be provoking different feelings in yourself than if you look at it in other ways.

Woman #3: So, how could she have handled that? The body language is excluding her, the conversation is excluding her. I mean, how does she get to her needs?

MBR: If her objective is to fully express her anger, I would suggest that she become conscious of this thing that we're struggling with now, that she become conscious of what she's telling herself that is making her so angry. So, in this case, it sounds like it's come out to be something like: She got angry because she immediately interpreted herself being excluded on the basis of race. This raises all kinds of thoughts in her, about that isn't right, you shouldn't exclude people on the basis of race—is that kind of deeply in there?

Woman #2: I think that came a little later. Yeah, my immediate experience is that I appear invisible and bewildered and confused. I don't understand why that's happening.

MBR: Yeah, so your immediate response in this case wasn't to judge the other person. The immediate one is that she's confused, bewildered. She has a need for some understanding, why is this happening? Then the thinking starts to go.

Woman #2: That's when the anger starts.

MBR: Then the anger starts to come because she starts to have some hypothesis about why this might be going on. And now it's that part we want to express fully, this anger that comes from interpreting: "Hey, wait a minute, I think this is excluding me on the basis of race and I don't like that. I think that's racist, I don't think that's fair. I don't think a person should be excluded on that basis." Thoughts like that.

Woman #2: Yeah.

MBR: OK, now that's the second step. First step, be quiet and identify the thoughts that are making us angry. Next, get connected to the needs behind those thoughts. So, when you say to yourself, "I don't think a person should be excluded on a basis of race, I think that's unfair, I think that's racist," I'm suggesting all judgments—and "racist" would be a good example—are tragic expressions of unmet needs. Now, what is the need behind the judgment *racist*? If I judge somebody as a racist, what is my need?

I would like to be included, I would like there to be equality. I would like to be given the same respect and consideration as anybody else. Now, to fully express my anger I open my mouth and say that, because now the anger has been transformed into my needs and need-connected feelings, but now the need-connected feelings for me are much scarier for me to express than the anger, you see.

"That was a racist thing to do." That is not hard for me to do at all. I kind of like to do that. But, it's really scary for me to get down to what's behind that, because feelings for me are so deeply related to racism that it's scary, but that's fully expressing the anger. So, then I might open my mouth and say to the person: "When you came into the group just now and started to talk to others and not say anything to me, and then when I heard the comment about white I felt really sick to my stomach and really scared. It just triggered off all kinds of needs on my part to be treated equally, and I'd like you to tell me how you feel when I tell you this.

Woman #2: Actually, I did have something like that conversation with the person. And some of my frustration and anger that doesn't go away is that I could get so far with that, but I get the feeling that there's this whole range of experience I've had that isn't comprehended.

MBR: So if I'm hearing you right, you're afraid that the other person is not going to really connect and understand all that's going on for you in that, all the experience for you in that?

Woman #2: Right. And then there's buildup over years of, you know, what I guess I would call rage about that gap.

Getting Understanding From Others About Our Feelings and Needs

MBR: We want to get some understanding from that person. So fully expressing the anger means not just that I express these deep feelings behind them, but I have to have this person get it.

Well, we've got to develop some skills for doing it. We've got to develop some skills, because you notice if I want understanding from such a person, the best way I can get the understanding that you're talking about is to give this person the understanding first. See, the more I empathize with what led this person to behave this way, the greater the likelihood that I'll be able afterward to get this person to reciprocate and hear all of this depth of experience that I have with them. It's going to be pretty hard for them to hear it. So, if I want them to hear it, I need to first empathize. Let me give you an idea of how that goes in a situation like this.

For the last thirty years, I've had a lot of experience with racism, because I started off with how to use NVC with people who have strong racial positions. Unfortunately to this day, in many of the countries that I work in, this is the number one thing that the citizens are concerned with. In many countries in the world skinheads and other groups of neo-fascists are making it very unsafe to move about. This is a very big issue, so we need to get very good at getting these people to understand.

So, I was in a cab one time. It was early in the morning and there was another person and me in the cab. It picked both of us up at the airport to take us into town and over the loud speaker for the cabbie we heard, "Pick up Mr. Fishman at the synagogue on such and such street." And the man sitting next to me said, "These kikes get up in the morning early so they can screw everybody out of their money."

I had smoke coming out of my ears, that's true, because it takes far less than that to make a maniac out of me. For many years my first reaction would have been to physically hurt this person. So, for about twenty seconds I had to take a deep breath and give myself some empathy for all the hurt, fear, rage and more that was going on in me. OK, so I listen to that. I'm conscious that my anger isn't coming from him; it's not coming from his statement. My anger, the depth of my fear, could not be stimulated by such a statement. It goes far deeper than that.

I know it has nothing to do with his statement; it just triggered me to want to blow up like a volcano. So, I sat back and just enjoyed this judgment show going on in my head, you know. I enjoyed the images of taking his head and smashing it. And then the first words out of my mouth were, "Are you feeling and needing?" I wanted to empathize with him. I wanted to hear his pain. Why? Because I wanted him to get it. I wanted him to see what was going on in me when he said that. But I've learned that if I want that kind of understanding of what goes on in me, other people cannot hear that if they've got a storm going on in them.

So, I want to connect and show a respectful empathy for the life energy in him that was behind that comment, because my experience tells me that when I do he's going to be able to hear me. It's not going to be easy, but he'll be able to hear me. So, I said, "It sounds like you had some bad experiences with Jewish people." And he looks at me. "Yeah," he said. "You know, these people are disgusting, they'll do anything for money." "Sounds like you have a lot of distrust and you need to protect yourself when you're with them about financial affairs." "Yes." So, he keeps going on with it. And I kept hearing his feelings and needs.

Now, you know, when you put your attention on other people's feelings and needs there's no conflict. Because what were his feelings and needs? When I hear that he's scared and wants to protect himself, I have those needs. I have a need to protect myself. I know what it's like to be scared. When my consciousness is on another human being's feelings and needs, I see the universality of all of our experience. I have a big conflict with what goes on in his head, his way of thinking. But I've learned that I enjoy human beings a lot better when I don't hear what they think. I've learned, especially with folks that have his kinds of thoughts, that I can enjoy life a lot better if I hear what's going on in their heart and not get caught up with that stuff that comes out of the head. So, really, after awhile this guy was just really pouring out his sadness and frustration. Before we know it he got off of Jews and now he's on to blacks and some other groups. The guy had a lot of pain about all kinds of stuff.

And then after maybe ten minutes of my just listening, he stopped. He felt understood. And then I let him know what was going on in me. I said: "You know, when you first started to talk I felt a lot of frustration, discouragement, because I've had quite different experience with Jews than you've had, and I was really wanting you to have much more the experience that I have. Can you tell me what you heard me say?" "Well, look, I'm not saying they're all . . ." I said: "Excuse me. Hold it, hold it. Could you tell me what you heard me say?" "What are you talking about?" "Let me say again what I'm trying to say. I want you to hear, really hear the pain that I felt when I heard your words. It's really important for me that you hear that. I said I felt a real sense of sadness because I've had such different experience with Jewish people and I was just wishing that you could share a different experience than you've had. Can you tell me what you've heard me say?"

"Well, you're saying I have no right to say that."

I replied: "No, I really don't want to blame you. Really, I don't have any desire to blame you."

See, to whatever degree he hears blame, he's not getting it. He's not getting it. Too easy. If he had said, "It was a terrible thing for me to say, that was a racist thing for me to say, I shouldn't have said it," he didn't get it. If he hears that he did anything wrong, he didn't get it. I want him to hear the pain that goes on in my heart when he says that. I want him to see what needs of mine do not get met when he says that. I do not want to blame him. That's too easy.

So, we have to work for that—we've got to pull the judging person by the ears. Here's why: People who judge are not too used to hearing feelings and needs. They're used to hearing blame and then they either agree with it and hate themselves, which doesn't stop them from continuing to behave that way, or they hate you for calling them a racist, which doesn't stop them from behaving that way. So, that's what I mean by needing the other person to get it. You may have to hear their pain for a while first. Well, let me say to you that before I could hear such people's pain, I had to do a lot of work for years before I could do it. A lot of work!

Woman #2: I still feel like I want to be able to protect myself. In other words, if I had a choice I just wouldn't interact with the person, but since they got in my space, I kind of got involved and so I'm not sure what you're trying to say.

MBR: What I'm saying is that if we want to fully express our anger to the person then I would go through this. But, I'm not saying *I always* want to fully express my anger to such a person. Very often my need might be to go talk to somebody else about this, to ignore this person. But if I really wanted to fully express my anger to them, I would give them the empathy that they would need to be able to hear the depth of feelings and needs that go on in me when that behavior occurs.

That's the best way I have found to really fully express my anger, to really let this person know the depth of what's going on in me. As you point out, it's not enough to just pour that out. I need them to get it; I need them to hear it, empathically. That doesn't mean they have to agree, they don't even have to change the behavior, I just need them to hear what goes on in me. So, for twenty seconds I had a whole lifetime of stuff floating in, and I sat back and enjoyed it.

Woman #3: How do you do that?

Enjoying the Judgment Show in Your Head

Here's what goes on in me. Not long ago I was in one country and somebody was coming at me pretty hard in a judging kind of way and here was my response. This person was going blah, blah, blah, blah, and saying some very judgmental things toward me and here was my reaction. [MBR is silent for a while.] "So, you're feeling really annoyed and you would have liked so and so." The person says, "Yes and blah, blah, blah." And here's my reaction. [MBR is silent again] "So, and it sounds like you were feeling some hurt behind that because you would have liked blah, blah, blah." "Yes, and blah, blah, blah."

Anyway, this went on several times and after this stopped a woman said to me: "Marshall, I've never seen a person more compassionate than you are. If somebody had talked to me the way that you were being talked to there I would've hit them. How did you do it?"

I said: "Let me tell you what was going on in me. You remember that first statement?" "Yes." "Here's my first reaction. If you don't shut up I'm going to jam your head up your #@$#. In fact, you've got your head so far up there, you need a cellophane navel to see."

And then I said to the woman: "And it got worse from there. I mean, then I had some real graphic images and I started to realize that this person's statements were very like some ridicule that I had experienced as a child. I realized that behind that I had a lot of fear and all of that. I went from this rage and wanting to shake her, to being aware of the humiliation behind that. I just stopped and listened. And when I got to that humiliation, that fear of being humiliated, I felt a release in my body. Then I could do what you heard me say, which is shift my attention and put my attention on her feelings and needs.

"And then you remember the second statement she hit me with?" And this other person said, "Yes." Then I said, "Here was my first reaction." And when I told her my first reaction, this woman's eyes get very big. She says, "I never knew you were so violent." So, I have gone from being very compassionate to very violent in just a couple of exchanges.

Well, they're both there. There's an enormous amount of violence in me conditioned by cultural factors and other things. So, I enjoy that. I just sit back when I get that angry and I just watch this violent show going on in my head. I hear all these violent things I'd like to say and I see these things I'd like to do to this person and then I listen to the pain that's behind it. And when I get to the pain behind it, there's always a release.

Then I can put my attention on the other person's humanness. I'm not repressing anything, quite the opposite. I'm enjoying it, this show going on, this violent show going in my head.

Woman #4: You're just not acting on it.

MBR: I'm just not acting on it because to act on it is too superficial. If I jump in and blame this person, we're never going to get down to the pain behind all this. I'm not going to really be able to fully express my needs to this person and have them get it. We'll just get into a fight and I know how that ends: Even when I win, I don't feel good. So, no, I want to fully express what's going on in me.

Take Your Time

Woman #5: You've mentioned before that this is a slow process. You mention you need time; you take time to give yourself empathy. Well, if you're trying to have a conversation, you know, to deal with that, it seems to me you have to tell the other person, "Well, what a minute. I'm thinking before I can answer." I mean, because you may think more slowly so you can respond.

MBR: Yes. I carry with me a picture of a son of a friend of mine. It was the last picture taken before he was killed in the battle of Lebanon. The reason I keep this picture with me is that, in the last picture, the son was wearing a T-shirt and the T-shirt said *Take Your Time*. And that's a very powerful symbol to me. It's probably the most important part for me in learning this process, learning how to live by it. Take your time. Yes, it feels awkward at times not to behave out of the automatic way I was trained, but I want to take my time so that I live my life in harmony with my own values instead of in a robot-like way, automatically carrying out the way I was programmed by the culture in which I was raised. So, yes, take your time. It may feel awkward, but for me it's my life. I'm going to take my time to live it in a way I want. I can look silly with that perhaps.

A friend of mine, Sam Williams, he put this process on a three-by-five card, the kind we're now selling—we got the idea from Sam. And he would use this as a cheat sheet at work, you see. The boss would come at him in a judging way, and he would take his time. He would stop and look down at this card in his hand and remember how to respond. And I said, "Sam, don't people think you're a little weird looking down at your hand and taking all of that time?" He said, "Actually, it doesn't take me that much time. But even so, I don't care. I want to really make sure that I'm responding as I want to respond." But at home he was overt about it. He explained to his children and to his wife why he had this card and he said, "I may look strange and I may take a lot of time, but this is why I'm doing it." So, when they would have these arguments at home he would take his time, but after about a month he felt comfortable enough to put card away. And then one night he and Scotty, age four, were having a conflict about the television and it wasn't going well and Scotty said, "Daddy, get the card."

Woman #7: Now, you sell these cards?

MBR: No, the Center for Nonviolent Communication does.

An Invitation

What's missing from this transcription is the experience of sharing time and space with Marshall Rosenberg or one of the CNVC certified trainers. The power, warmth, and poignancy of the NVC message are amplified by being at a training in person. The interplay with a live audience adds a dimension to the learning process that is hard to match on paper. If you'd like to see Marshall or another CNVC trainer in person, please visit www.CNVC.org for a schedule of NVC trainings and speaking engagements, and a listing of NVC Trainers and Support People around the world.

For a complete up-to-date listing of all NVC materials—audios, CDs, books, and more—please visit www.CNVC.org. For additional NVC information, please visit www.Nonviolent Communication.com.

Anger Sound Bites

- How I choose to look at that situation will greatly affect whether I have the power to change it or make matters worse.

- There's not a thing another person can do that can make us angry.

- Any thinking that is in your head that involves the word *should* is violence provoking.

- I don't think we get angry because our needs aren't getting met. I think we get angry because we have judgments about others.

- Anger is a natural feeling created by unnatural thinking.

- I'm not saying that it is wrong to judge people . . . what's important is to be conscious that it's that judgment that makes us angry.

- Even if you don't say judgments out loud, your eyes show this kind of thinking.

- Use the words *I feel because I* . . . to remind us that what we feel it is not because of what the other person did, but because of the choice I made.

- To me the life that's going on within us can be most clearly grasped by looking at what our needs are. Ask yourself, "What are my needs in this situation?"

- When I am connected to my needs I have strong feelings, but never anger. I see all anger as a result of life-alienated, violent, provocative thinking.

- Killing people is too superficial. To me, any kind of killing, blaming of other people, hurting of other people, is a very superficial expression of our anger.

- Our aim is to keep our attention, moment by moment, connected to life, the life that's going on in us. What are our needs at this moment, and what's alive in others?

- Sadness is a feeling that mobilizes us to get our needs met. Anger is a feeling that mobilizes us to blame and punish others.

- Fully expressing the anger means not that I just express these deep feelings behind it, but to have this person get it.

- To fully express the anger means getting our full consciousness on the need that isn't getting met.

- The best way I can get understanding from another person . . . is to give this person the understanding, too. If I want them to hear my needs and feelings, I first need to empathize.

- When I give people the empathy they need, I haven't found it is that hard to get them to hear me.

- Anger is a very valuable feeling in NVC. It's a wake-up call. It tells us that I'm thinking in ways almost guaranteed not to meet my needs. Why? Because my energy is not connected to my needs, and I'm not even aware of what my needs are when I'm angry.

The Four-Part Nonviolent Communication Process

Clearly expressing how **I am** without blaming or criticizing	Empathically receiving how **you are** without hearing blame or criticism

OBSERVATIONS

1. What I observe *(see, hear, remember, imagine, free from my evaluations)* that does or does not contribute to my well-being:

   "When I (see, hear) . . . "

1. What you observe *(see, hear, remember, imagine, free from your evaluations)* that does or does not contribute to your well-being:

   "When you see/hear . . . "

   (Sometimes unspoken when offering empathy)

FEELINGS

2. How I feel *(emotion or sensation rather than thought)* in relation to what I observe:

   "I feel . . . "

2. How you feel *(emotion or sensation rather than thought)* in relation to what you observe:

   "You feel . . ."

NEEDS

3. What I need or value *(rather than a preference, or a specific action)* that causes my feelings:

   " . . . because I need/value . . . "

3. What you need or value *(rather than a preference, or a specific action)* that causes your feelings:

   " . . . because you need/value . . ."

Clearly requesting that which would enrich **my** life without demanding	Empathically receiving that which would enrich **your** life without hearing any demand

REQUESTS

4. The concrete actions I would like taken:

   "Would you be willing to . . . ?"

4. The concrete actions you would like taken:

   "Would you like . . . ?"

   (Sometimes unspoken when offering empathy)

© Marshall B. Rosenberg. For more information about Marshall B. Rosenberg or the Center for Nonviolent Communication, please visit www.CNVC.org.

Some Basic Feelings We All Have

Feelings when needs are fulfilled

- Amazed
- Comfortable
- Confident
- Eager
- Energetic
- Fulfilled
- Glad
- Hopeful
- Inspired
- Intrigued
- Joyous
- Moved
- Optimistic
- Proud
- Relieved
- Stimulated
- Surprised
- Thankful
- Touched
- Trustful

Feelings when needs are not fulfilled

- Angry
- Annoyed
- Concerned
- Confused
- Disappointed
- Discouraged
- Distressed
- Embarrassed
- Frustrated
- Helpless
- Hopeless
- Impatient
- Irritated
- Lonely
- Nervous
- Overwhelmed
- Puzzled
- Reluctant
- Sad
- Uncomfortable

Some Basic Needs We All Have

Autonomy
- Choosing dreams/goals/values
- Choosing plans for fulfilling one's dreams, goals, values

Celebration
- Celebrating the creation of life and dreams fulfilled
- Celebrating losses: loved ones, dreams, etc. (mourning)

Integrity
- Authenticity • Creativity
- Meaning • Self-worth

Interdependence
- Acceptance • Appreciation
- Closeness • Community
- Consideration
- Contribution to the enrichment of life
- Emotional Safety • Empathy

Physical Nurturance
- Air • Food
- Movement, exercise
- Protection from life-threatening forms of life: viruses, bacteria, insects, predatory animals
- Rest • Sexual Expression
- Shelter • Touch • Water

Play
- Fun • Laughter

Spiritual Communion
- Beauty • Harmony
- Inspiration • Order • Peace
- Honesty (the empowering honesty that enables us to learn from our limitations)
- Love • Reassurance
- Respect • Support
- Trust • Understanding

About PuddleDancer Press

PuddleDancer Press (PDP) is the main publisher of Nonviolent Communication™ related works. Its mission is to provide high-quality materials to help people create a world in which all needs are met compassionately. By working in partnership with the Center for Nonviolent Communication and NVC trainers, teams, and local supporters, PDP has created a comprehensive promotion effort that has helped bring NVC to thousands of new people each year.

Since 1998 PDP has donated more than 60,000 NVC books to organizations, decision-makers, and individuals in need around the world.

Visit the PDP website at www.NonviolentCommunication.com to find the following resources:

- **Shop NVC**—Continue your learning. Purchase our NVC titles online safely, affordably, and conveniently. Find everyday discounts on individual titles, multiple-copies, and book packages. Learn more about our authors and read endorsements of NVC from world-renowned communication experts and peacemakers. www.NonviolentCommunication.com/store/

- **NVC Quick Connect e-Newsletter**—Sign up today to receive our monthly e-Newsletter, filled with expert articles, upcoming training opportunities with our authors, and exclusive specials on NVC learning materials. Archived e-Newsletters are also available

- **About NVC**—Learn more about these life-changing communication and conflict resolution skills including an overview of the NVC process, key facts about NVC, and more.

- **About Marshall Rosenberg**—Access press materials, biography, and more about this world-renowned peacemaker, educator, bestselling author, and founder of the Center for Nonviolent Communication.

- **Free Resources for Learning NVC**—Find free weekly tips series, NVC article archive, and other great resources to make learning these vital communication skills just a little easier.

For more information, please contact PuddleDancer Press at:

2240 Encinitas Blvd., Ste. D-911 • Encinitas, CA 92024
Phone: 760-652-5754 • Fax: 760-274-6400
Email: email@puddledancer.com • www.NonviolentCommunication.com

About Nonviolent Communication

Nonviolent Communication has flourished for more than four decades across sixty countries selling more than 1,000,000 books in over thirty languages for one simple reason: it works.

From the bedroom to the boardroom, from the classroom to the war zone, Nonviolent Communication (NVC) is changing lives every day. NVC provides an easy-to-grasp, effective method to get to the root of violence and pain peacefully. By examining the unmet needs behind what we do and say, NVC helps reduce hostility, heal pain, and strengthen professional and personal relationships. NVC is now being taught in corporations, classrooms, prisons, and mediation centers worldwide. And it is affecting cultural shifts as institutions, corporations, and governments integrate NVC consciousness into their organizational structures and their approach to leadership.

Most of us are hungry for skills that can improve the quality of our relationships, to deepen our sense of personal empowerment or simply help us communicate more effectively. Unfortunately, most of us have been educated from birth to compete, judge, demand, and diagnose; to think and communicate in terms of what is "right" and "wrong" with people. At best, the habitual ways we think and speak hinder communication and create misunderstanding or frustration. And still worse, they can cause anger and pain, and may lead to violence. Without wanting to, even people with the best of intentions generate needless conflict.

NVC helps us reach beneath the surface and discover what is alive and vital within us, and how all of our actions are based on human needs that we are seeking to meet. We learn to develop a vocabulary of feelings and needs that helps us more clearly express what is going on in us at any given moment. When we understand and acknowledge our needs, we develop a shared foundation for much more satisfying relationships. Join the thousands of people worldwide who have improved their relationships and their lives with this simple yet revolutionary process.

The Center for Nonviolent Communication (CNVC) is an international nonprofit peacemaking organization whose vision is a world where everyone's needs are met peacefully. CNVC is devoted to supporting the spread of Nonviolent Communication (NVC) around the world.

Founded in 1984 by Dr. Marshall B. Rosenberg, CNVC has been contributing to a vast social transformation in thinking, speaking and acting—showing people how to connect in ways that inspire compassionate results. NVC is now being taught around the globe in communities, schools, prisons, mediation centers, churches, businesses, professional conferences, and more. Hundreds of certified trainers and hundreds more supporters teach NVC to tens of thousands of people each year in more than 60 countries.

CNVC believes that NVC training is a crucial step to continue building a compassionate, peaceful society. Your tax-deductible donation will help CNVC continue to provide training in some of the most impoverished, violent corners of the world. It will also support the development and continuation of organized projects aimed at bringing NVC training to high-need geographic regions and populations.

To make a tax-deductible donation or to learn more about the valuable resources described below, visit the CNVC website at www.CNVC.org:

- **Training and Certification**—Find local, national, and international training opportunities, access trainer certification information, connect to local NVC communities, trainers, and more.

- **CNVC Bookstore**—Find mail or phone order information for a complete selection of NVC books, booklets, audio, and video materials at the CNVC website.

- **CNVC Projects**—Participate in one of the several regional and theme-based projects that provide focus and leadership for teaching NVC in a particular application or geographic region.

- **E-Groups and List Servs**—Join one of several moderated, topic-based NVC e-groups and list servs developed to support individual learning and the continued growth of NVC worldwide.

For more information, please contact CNVC at:

9301 Indian School Rd., NE, Suite 204, Albuquerque, NM 87112-2861
Ph: 505-244-4041 • US Only: 800-255-7696 • Fax: 505-247-0414
Email: cnvc@CNVC.org • Website: www.CNVC.org

Nonviolent Communication:
A Language of Life, 3rd Edition

Life-Changing Tools for Healthy Relationships

Marshall B. Rosenberg, PhD

$19.95 – Trade Paper 6x9, 264pp
ISBN: 978-1-892005-28-1

What is "Violent" Communication?

If "violent" means acting in ways that result in hurt or harm, then much of how we communicate—judging others, bullying, having racial bias, blaming, finger pointing, discriminating, speaking without listening, criticizing others or ourselves, name-calling, reacting when angry, using political rhetoric, being defensive or judging who's "good/bad" or what's "right/wrong" with people—could indeed be called "violent communication."

What is "Nonviolent" Communication?

Nonviolent Communication is the integration of 4 things:

Consciousness: a set of principles that support living a life of empathy, care, courage, and authenticity

Language: understanding how words contribute to connection or distance

Communication: knowing how to ask for what we want, how to hear others even in disagreement, and how to move toward solutions that work for all

Means of influence: sharing "power with others" rather than using "power over others"

Nonviolent Communication
Companion Workbook, 2nd Edition

A Practical Guide for Individual, Group, or Classroom Study

by Lucy Leu

$21.95 – Trade Paper 7x10, 240pp
ISBN: 978-1-892005-29-8

Learning Nonviolent Communication has often been equated with learning a whole new language. The *NVC Companion Workbook* helps you put these powerful, effective skills into practice with chapter-by-chapter study of Marshall Rosenberg's cornerstone text, *NVC: A Language of Life.* Create a safe, supportive group learning or practice environment that nurtures the needs of each participant. Find a wealth of activities, exercises, and facilitator suggestions to refine and practice this powerful communication process.

Nonviolent Communication has flourished for more than four decades across sixty countries selling more than 1,000,000 books for a simple reason: it works.

Available from PuddleDancer Press, the Center for Nonviolent Communication, all major bookstores, and Amazon.com. Distributed by Independent Publisher's Group: 800-888-4741.

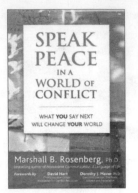

Speak Peace in a World of Conflict

What You Say Next Will Change Your World

by Marshall B. Rosenberg, PhD

$15.95 – Trade Paper 5-3/8x8-3/8, 208pp
ISBN: 978-1-892005-17-5

International peacemaker, mediator, and healer, Marshall Rosenberg shows you how the language you use is the key to enriching life. *Speak Peace* is filled with inspiring stories, lessons, and ideas drawn from more than forty years of mediating conflicts and healing relationships in some of the most war-torn, impoverished, and violent corners of the world. Find insight, practical skills, and powerful tools that will profoundly change your relationships and the course of your life for the better.

Discover how you can create an internal consciousness of peace as the first step toward effective personal, professional, and social change. Find complete chapters on the mechanics of Speaking Peace, conflict resolution, transforming business culture, transforming enemy images, addressing terrorism, transforming authoritarian structures, expressing and receiving gratitude, and social change.

SAVE an extra 10% at NonviolentCommunication.com with code: **bookads**

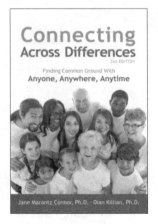

Connecting Across Differences,

2nd Edition

Finding Common Ground With Anyone, Anywhere, Anytime

by Jane Marantz Connor, PhD and Dian Killian, PhD

$19.95 – Trade Paper 6x9, 416pp
ISBN: 978-1-892005-24-3

Profound Connection Is Just a Conversation Away!

In this fully revised second edition, Dr. Dian Killian and Dr. Jane Marantz Connor offer an accessible guide for exploring the concepts, applications, and transformative power of the Nonviolent Communication process. Discover simple, yet transformative skills to create a life of abundance, building the personal, professional, and community connections you long for.

Now with an expanded selection of broadly applicable exercises, role-plays, and activities. Detailed and comprehensive, this combined book and workbook enhances communication skills by introducing the basic NVC model, as well as more advanced NVC practices.

Available from PuddleDancer Press, the Center for Nonviolent Communication, all major bookstores, and Amazon.com. Distributed by Independent Publisher's Group: 800-888-4741.

Being Me, Loving You: *A Practical Guide to Extraordinary Relationships* **by Marshall B. Rosenberg, PhD** • Watch your relationships strengthen as you learn to think of love as something you "do," something you give freely from the heart.
80pp, ISBN: 978-1-892005-16-8 • **$6.95**

Getting Past the Pain Between Us: *Healing and Reconciliation Without Compromise* **by Marshall B. Rosenberg, PhD** • Learn simple steps to create the heartfelt presence necessary for lasting healing to occur—great for mediators, counselors, families, and couples.
48pp, ISBN: 978-1-892005-07-6 • **$6.95**

Graduating From Guilt: *Six Steps to Overcome Guilt and Reclaim Your Life* **by Holly Michelle Eckert** • The burden of guilt leaves us stuck, stressed, and feeling like we can never measure up. Through a proven six-step process, this book helps liberate you from the toxic guilt, blame, and shame you carry.
96pp, ISBN: 978-1-892005-23-6 • **$9.95**

The Heart of Social Change: *How to Make a Difference in Your World* **by Marshall B. Rosenberg, PhD** • Learn how creating an internal consciousness of compassion can impact your social change efforts.
48pp, ISBN: 978-1-892005-10-6 • **$8.95**

Humanizing Health Care: *Creating Cultures of Compassion With Nonviolent Communication* **by Melanie Sears, RN, MBA** • Leveraging more than 25 years nursing experience, Melanie demonstrates the profound effectiveness of NVC to create lasting, positive improvements to patient care and the health care workplace.
112pp, ISBN: 978-1-892005-26-7 • **$9.95**

Parenting From Your Heart: *Sharing the Gifts of Compassion, Connection, and Choice* **by Inbal Kashtan** • Filled with insight and practical skills, this booklet will help you transform your parenting to address every day challenges.
48pp, ISBN: 978-1-892005-08-3 • **$8.95**

Practical Spirituality: *Reflections on the Spiritual Basis of Nonviolent Communication* **by Marshall B. Rosenberg, PhD** • Marshall's views on the spiritual origins and underpinnings of NVC, and how practicing the process helps him connect to the Divine.
48pp, ISBN: 978-1-892005-14-4 • **$8.95**

Raising Children Compassionately: *Parenting the Nonviolent Communication Way* **by Marshall B. Rosenberg, PhD** • Learn to create a mutually respectful, enriching family dynamic filled with heartfelt communication.
32pp, ISBN: 978-1-892005-09-0 • **$7.95**

The Surprising Purpose of Anger: *Beyond Anger Management: Finding the Gift* **by Marshall B. Rosenberg, PhD** • Marshall shows you how to use anger to discover what you need, and then how to meet your needs in more constructive, healthy ways.
48pp, ISBN: 978-1-892005-15-1 • **$6.95**

Teaching Children Compassionately: *How Students and Teachers Can Succeed With Mutual Understanding* **by Marshall B. Rosenberg, PhD** • In this national keynote address to Montessori educators, Marshall describes his progressive, radical approach to teaching that centers on compassionate connection.
48pp, ISBN: 978-1-892005-11-3 • **$6.95**

We Can Work It Out: *Resolving Conflicts Peacefully and Powerfully* **by Marshall B. Rosenberg, PhD** • Practical suggestions for fostering empathic connection, genuine co-operation, and satisfying resolutions in even the most difficult situations.
32pp, ISBN: 978-1-892005-12-0 • **$7.95**

What's Making You Angry? *10 Steps to Transforming Anger So Everyone Wins* **by Shari Klein and Neill Gibson** • A powerful, step-by-step approach to transform anger to find healthy, mutually satisfying outcomes.
32pp, ISBN: 978-1-892005-13-7 • **$7.95**

Available from PuddleDancer Press, the Center for Nonviolent Communication, all major bookstores, and Amazon.com. Distributed by IPG: 800-888-4741. For more information about these booklets or to order online, visit www.NonviolentCommunication.com